TYNESIDE: THEN AND NOW

Geoff Phillips

Published by G P Electronic Services
87 Willowtree Avenue, Durham City, DH1 1DZ.
Tel: 0191 384 9707
Email: geoff1946@aol.com
Website http://books.north-east.co.uk

ISBN 0 9540174 2 0

Front cover design by Geoff Phillips
Main text, interior design, typesetting,
and graphics by Geoff Phillips.

Modern photographs by Geoff Phillips and Craig Oliphant
Old Photographs by Jack Phillips, Steve Wood, Stanley Victor Walton, and Jim Perry

Printed by: Blamire Printers, Ferryhill, Co Durham

Acknowledgments:
Many thanks go to:
David Lovie - Historic Areas Advisor, English Heritage, for writing the Foreword and for his valuable contributions to the text.
Thanks also to Jim Perry, Steve Wood, Iain McKay, Darren Scott, and Dorothy Rand,

Special thanks go to my wife June for painstakingly checking the text.

Details and pictures from other books by Geoff Phillips
may be seen at our website
http://books.north-east.co.uk

Bibliography:
The History of Newcastle upon Tyne - Henry Bourne 1736
A History of Newcastle-on-Tyne - R J Charleton , 1893.
The Buildings of Grainger Town - David Lovie, 1997.
Northern City: An Architectural History of Newcastle upon Tyne - Lynn Pearson, 1996.
Newcastle upon Tyne - Peter Winter, David Milne, Jonathan Brown, Alan Rushworth.
What's in a Name - Anna Flowers, Maria Hoy, 1992.
Newcastle - Frank Graham (revised edition 1995).
Heady Days; A History of Newcastle's Public Houses - Brian Bennison, 1996
The Cinemas of Newcastle - Frank Manders, 1991
Ghosts of Graingertown - Vanessa Histon, 2001

TYNESIDE: THEN AND NOW

Geoff Phillips

Tyne river, running rough or smooth,
Brings bread to me and mine;
Of all the rivers north or south
There's none like coaly Tyne.

- Local song

Foreword by David Lovie
Historic Areas Advisor at English Heritage

More Pictures

One of my favourite sayings that I love to bore my friends and colleagues with is: "The one constant is change!" The truth of this useful little adage is demonstrated on every page of Geoff Phillips' latest book of pictures. Although the NOW illustrations are usually easy to recognise, the THEN pictures may be far from familiar. Geoff even finds it necessary for many of the locations in the book, to assist the reader to relate THEN to NOW by pointing out the surviving visual links that connect them.
Truly, change is a constant.

But, although change may be the general name of the game, it has been estimated that at least 70% of our urban surroundings are at least 50 years old - unless, of course, you live in a New Town like Cramlington or Washington where virtually everything is modern. For the rest of us, 70% of our surroundings are old.

Should we be grateful for this historic continuity in our surroundings? Well, in the conservation business we recognise that retaining the best of out built legacy helps to give us all a sense of stability in our lives and encourages a passionate pride, not only in the glories (and little half-remembered details) of our national and local past but in the potential richness of our future. This is why we need to work hard to secure a future for our past

---

European Capital of Culture 2008 - Newcastle/Gateshead bid

Since the bid went in earlier this year, all Tyneside has been buzzing with this word "Culture". It is one of those useful words that is sufficiently ambiguous (and grandiose) as to cover all occasions, events, features, activities etc. involving local colour or national taste.

So, this North East produced book also makes a contribution to the current cultural ferment on Tyneside. But, exactly what cultural issues does it illustrate?

First, it presents our historic buildings, our Tyneside heritage, as an essential part of our local way of life, pride and culture. The ever present built legacy of past "cultures" continue to inform our present existence. Secondly, Geoff has such an insatiable appetite for many popular cultural elements of past and present Tyneside life, it is inevitable that many illustrations of them found their way into this book.

The whole range of popular music is represented by Balmbra's Music Hall, the old Oxford Galleries and all kinds of street music in Grey Street, while cinema and theatre include the old Flora Robson Playhouse, the Newcastle Picture House in Grey Street and the excellent Paramount/Odean cinema in Pilgrim Street. Newcastle's pub culture is well represented too: ancient Bourgogne's, the Quayside's Barley Mow, The Tyne (now Waterside) and last but not least, Newcastle's curiously named Egypt Cottage. Popular cultural activities like the traditional Hoppings, the medieval Quayside Market and "messing about in boats" on the Ouseburn are also given a place. In fact, almost all of Tyneside's rich cultural legacy is presented in this single book.

We are grateful to Geoff Phillips for this new book which further chronicles the cultural changes of Tyneside. It is essential reading for all citizens of the aspiring European Capital of Culture on both banks of the Tyne.

Contents

A Walk Around Newcastle

If you are intrigued by the 'then and now' photographs in this book, you may wish to visit the scenes for yourself. A walking route around the streets of Newcastle has been devised which enables the interested reader to see the views of the city, in the same order as they appear in this book. It should be pointed out that the walk is of considerable distance and some may wish not to cover the entire route in one day. Parts of the walk are not suitable for wheelchairs, also there are views of the suburbs of Tyneside in this book which are not covered by the walk.

The route starts at Newcastle's Quayside. If you are travelling to Newcastle by car you will find car parks all along the Quayside downstream from the Tyne Bridge. Parking here will be impossible on a Sunday morning when the traditional Quayside market is held, but there is free off-street parking in Newcastle on Sundays.

Views 1, 2 and 3 were taken on the Quayside which has undergone an amazing transformation in the last few decades as the pairs of photographs show. Decrepit warehouses and factories have been replaced by up-market apartments, prestigious offices, restaurants, leisure centres and public art. Take time to walk along the Quayside to observe the artworks which are part of the

"Art on the Riverside" project - the largest programme of public art in the UK.

The most obvious addition to the scene is the Gateshead Millennium Bridge linking Gateshead Quays to Newcastle's Quayside. The unique tilting design pedestrian and cycle bridge operates like the giant lid of an eye slowly opening, forming an arch under which ships can pass. A single opening or closing takes four minutes. The bridge was opened for cyclists and pedestrian traffic on Monday 17 September 2001 and was officially opened by Queen Elizabeth II on 7 May 2002. Take time to walk across the bridge to Gateshead Quays and visit Baltic Centre for Contemporary Art. The Baltic was originally a grain warehouse being part of the Baltic Flour Mills complex completed in 1950 for Joseph Rank Ltd. The complex closed in 1982 and all the buildings were demolished except for the grain warehouse which was left standing due to the prohibitive costs of destruction. In 1992 Gateshead Council commissioned an investigation into the feasibility of converting the warehouse into an arts centre. In 1997 the Arts Council awarded £33.4m from the National Lottery for the conversion of the Grain Warehouse into an international arts venue. The centre was opened on Saturday 13 July 2002 and houses over 3000 square metres of art space with five galleries, artists' studios, a

Gateshead Millennium Bridge

cinema / lecture theatre, a library and archive for the study of contemporary art, an art shop, and three food and drink spaces. Entrance is free and it is well worth a visit.

Views 4 and 5 were taken from the Tyne Bridge itself which was opened in 1928 and has always been the icon of Tyneside, but that status is now challenged by the Millennium Bridge. There is a lift from the Quayside to the road-deck of the Tyne Bridge which is in the east stone tower of the bridge.

Return to the Quayside and walk in a westerly direction along the quay and watch out for the Casa bar next to the Swing Bridge. This bar has been used as a set in many television productions such as "Auf Wiedersehen Pet", "Badger", and Newcastle's very own, but short-lived soap called "Quayside". On the other side of the Swing Bridge is a small stone building which was depicted as the offices of the law firm in the television drama "Close and True" starring James Bolam and Robson Green.

Turn right and walk north until you come to the Close, one of Newcastle's oldest streets which was reclaimed from the River Tyne between the 13th and 15th centuries. Walk east along the Close until you come to Sandhill and an eighteenth century building which was Bessie Surtees' house (view 6) The story about Bessie Surtees is detailed on page 22.

The large apsidal building in Sandhill (on the left of view 6) is the Guildhall, the inside of which remains from a previous building of 1658, and was the ancient centre of municipal government of the town. However, no part of the original building is now visible from the outside.

The route now takes you north, up the curved street called Side. Before you reach the railway arch you will see the Side Gallery on your left which usually has interesting historical photographs on view, and is well worth a visit. Entrance is free and there are picture postcards of local scenes on sale. Here are views 7 and 8. Walk under the railway arch, keep right and you are now in Dean Street. Notice Milburn House on the corner of Side and Dean Street. This building was depicted as the Police Headquarters in the BBC Television drama "Badger". Continue up Dean Street and look across the street to admire the lovely Cathedral Buildings.

The route now crosses Mosley Street and continues up Grey Street. You are now in Grainger Town, an historic area of Newcastle which was built in the 1830's by local builder Richard Grainger. A Traveller of the day described Mr Grainger's scheme as transforming medieval ~~tle~~ into a "City of Palaces". For many decades

EARL GREY'S MONUMENT

the fine stone Georgian Architecture of this part of Newcastle was black due to smoke pollution from the industry on Tyneside. Gradually the buildings have been cleaned and restored to their former glory. As you walk up Grey Street take time to admire the architecture of what was described by Prime Minister William Gladstone in 1862 as "Britain's best modern street". As you come to the top of Grey Street you will see views 9, 10 and 11, the elegant Theatre Royal and Grey's Monument. During the summer months there are often street musicians giving performances on the pedestrian area around Grey's Monument (view 12). View 13 may be seen by looking east along Blackett Street.

The walk now continues west along Blackett Street where you will see Eldon Square and views 14 and 16. To see view 15 you must take a temporary diversion through Eldon Square Shopping Centre's entrance opposite Fenwicks. Head for the post office and emerge from the centre onto Clayton Street. Clayton Street used to continue and join up with Blackett Street and Eldon Square before the shopping centre was built in the 1970's.

Retrace your steps onto Blackett Street, pass under the glass and steel structure which straddles the street and you come to the junction of Blackett Street and Percy Street and view 17. The ancient houses and shops seen in view 17 met their demise in the 1960's when IBM built a new office block, the ground floor of which was occupied by Barclays Bank. Head south along Newgate Street and you will come to St Andrews Church, said to be the oldest church in Newcastle and the possible location of the original Norman settlement which was the beginning of Newcastle. View 18 was taken from the corner of Newgate Street and Gallowgate and shows Bourgognes public house. Built in 1634, the building was originally the town jailer's house, but was bought by a French wine merchant, Bourgogne et Fils, in the 1870's. The pub was demolished in the 1970's amid much controversy as another piece of Newcastle's history was torn down in the name of progress. A new pub bearing the same name may be seen further south along Newgate Street.

Continue south along Newgate Street passing the magnificent Co-op building on your right and you will come to the junction with Clayton Street and view 19. View 20 may be seen further south on Newgate Street. Cross Grainger Street and you will enter Bigg Market. At the corner you will see the memorial fountain to the temperance reformer, Dr J H Rutherford who proclaimed 'Water is best'. The monument is probably aptly sited as this part of town has been the boozy centre of Newcastle for generations of Geordies. Standing close to the monument you will see view 21. Views 22 (a) and (b) were taken inside Balmbra's on the Cloth Market which is where Geordie Ridley first sang his song "Blaydon Races"

Retrace your steps along Newgate Street to Newcastle's new entertainment and leisure centre -"The Gate". Notice the cross of white stones set into the cobbles of the mini roundabout opposite. This denotes the position of a market cross called the White Cross which was built in 1784 to replace an older structure of the same name. The

Rutherford Memorial Fountain

cross marked that part of town where medieval markets were held and civic dignitaries would make proclamations. The cross was removed in 1808.

Cross Newgate Street and pass under "The Gate" into Low Friar Street. Turn right at Dispensary Lane and after a few metres you will enter the grounds of Blackfriars, the restored monastery of the Dominican Friars founded in the 13th century. Sir Peter Scott, an early Lord Mayor of Newcastle upon Tyne, is said to have funded the building of the monastery in the west of Newcastle just inside where the Town Wall was later built. Views 23 and 24 show the monastery before and after restoration by the City Council. The buildings now house craft shops and a restaurant. Walk through the arch in the Blackfriars buildings to emerge at Friars Street. Turn left, and then turn right along a narrow lane which leads you to Charlotte Square and Cross

Blackfriars

St Thomas Church
Haymarket

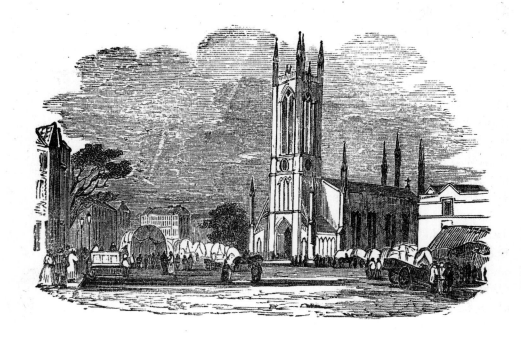

Street. Walk straight ahead down Cross Street and turn right onto Westgate Road where you will see views 25 and 26. One of the few remaining stretches of the Town Walls may be seen on Bath Lane. On Westgate Road you will also see Newcastle Opera House which was built in the 1860's but has been beautifully restored and is still a venue for music productions and pantomimes at Christmas.

Continue up Westgate Road until you meet the junction with Newcastle's new western thoroughfare, St James Boulevard. Look down Westgate Road to see view 27. Turn left and walk along the Boulevard to see view 28.

Make a U-turn and head north along St James Boulevard until you come to Newcastle United Football Club's impressive stadium - St James Park. On the opposite side of the Boulevard is a statue of Jackie Milburn, Tyneside's famous football hero, who led "The Toon" to three FA Cup victories in the 1950's. Views 29, 30, 31, and 32 were taken out of town on the West Road.

Turn right at St James' Park football stadium and walk down Gallowgate until you come to the junction with Percy Street and Blackett Street where you will see view 33, Eldon Square Shopping Centre. Turn left into Percy Street and continue until you pass underneath Eldon Gardens which straddles Percy Street. You will see a rotunda shaped car park on your right after which is where views 34 and 35 were taken.

Cross over Percy Street to see view No 36, Haymarket bus station. Walk north along Percy Street and you will see St Thomas Church, the South African War Memorial and the controversial water feature and soldier sculpture (View 37). The sculpture comprises 52 concrete figures which surround the memorial built in memory of the Newcastle men who lost their lives in the Boer War. The water feature did not win the hearts of Novocastrians and, at the time of writing, is earmarked to be given away to any organisation who could give it a good home. (View 38 was taken at the Town Moor which is a mile north of the city.)

Cross Percy Street at the pelican crossing and look towards the bus station to see view No 39. Continue walking with the Metro station on your left and then turn right into Northumberland Street to see view 40 - Vine Lane. Northumberland Street is Newcastle's answer to London's Oxford Street and is the shopper's "Mecca". All the retail giants are here along with department stores and fast food outlets. Views 41 and 42 were taken from the north end of Northumberland Street. Walk south and you will soon come to the junction with Northumberland Road. A few yards along Northumberland Road you will find, set into the BHS department store's north facing wall, an interesting mural which details the most significant events in Newcastle's history. Continue walking south down the normally crowded Northumberland Street and try to imagine that it used to carry the main north-south A1 road traffic as well as pedestrians. Halfway down the street is view 43 which shows four stone figures set into the building which was originally constructed for Boots the Chemist but is now scheduled to become part of Fenwick's department store. Continue south along Northumberland Street to the junction with New Bridge Street, Blackett Street and Pilgrim street to see views 44 - 47.

The route now continues east along New Bridge Street and when you come to John Dobson Street you will see views 48 and 49. View 48(a) was actually taken from the concrete deck which used to exist above John Dobson Street until it was demolished in the late 1990's. View 48(b) was taken from the balcony of the Central Library and shows the new premises of the Newcastle Building Society. They harmonise well with 19th century architect John Dobson's design for the Lying In Hospital, seen in the centre of the photograph. A lying-in hospital was a

Lying-in Hospital

maternity hospital for the poor, an institution which was founded in 1760. This particular hospital was opened in 1826 and helped bring over 1000 new babies a year into the world for nearly 100 years before closing in 1923. In 1925 the building was leased to the BBC for use as radio and television studios until 1988 when they moved to the "Pink Palace" in Spital Tongues.

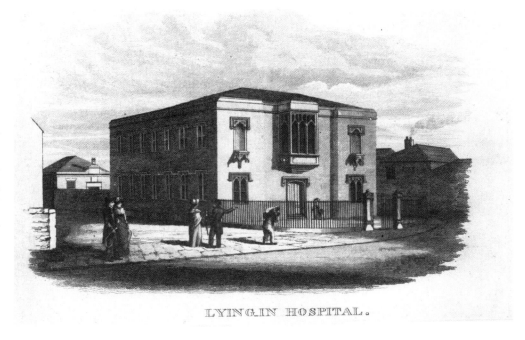

LYING-IN HOSPITAL.

Continue east along New Bridge Street, past the Central Library on your left, and cross John Dobson Street. You arrive at the Laing Art Gallery "Piazza" and the Blue Carpet - Views 50 and 51. The Blue Carpet is a work of public art which was designed by the Thomas Heatherwick Studio. It was the winning entry in a public competition launched by Newcastle City Council in July 1996 in partnership with local business, Northern Arts, and Tyne and Wear Museums. The tiles are made from a durable white resin mixed with recycled glass shards giving a shimmering effect of cool blues.

The Laing Art Gallery, completed in 1904, always has exhibits of paintings, watercolours, costume, silver, glass, pottery, and sculpture. Entrance is free.

To the east of the Laing is Higham Place which was Richard Grainger's first major building project in Newcastle. Walk further east and you will come to a nightclub called Ikon. This was originally the Oxford Galleries dance hall opened in 1926. To the left of the main entrance is the house where John Dobson lived from the 1820's to 1865. Views 52 (a) and (b) were taken inside Ikon.

Views 53 were taken further east along New Bridge Street but a hotel now blocks the route. In order to see views 53 and 54, walk along the alleyway (now called Oxford Street) to the right of Ikon. At the rear of Ikon is a narrow opening which leads to Durant Road. Walk east along Durant Road towards the large roundabout and you will come to the spot where views 53 and 54 were taken.

Cross Durant Road and head west until you see the path on your right leading to the church of the Divine Unity in what used to be Ellison Place. Extensions to the University of Northumbria have almost

Higham Place, Grainger's first Major Building Project in Newcastle

Photo: Jack Phillips 1965

Sally-Port or Carpenters Tower

Photo: Jack Phillips 1950's

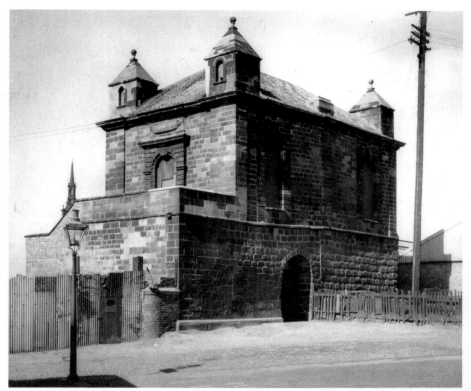

obliterated Ellison Place which used to be a quiet and elegant part of the City where Newcastle's Lord Mayor, the clergy and assize court judges resided in the nineteenth century. View 55(a) was actually taken from the north-west corner of the church looking south, but a pedestrian bridge now obscures the modern day view. I have taken the modern view from the east end of the church which makes a much more dramatic effect as the modern view now depicts the Central Motorway East.

Retrace your steps back to the Blue Carpet and climb Thomas Heatherwick's spiral staircase next to the Holiday Inn. The route now takes you east along a series of pedestrian bridges across the Central Motorway East. Head towards the Stout Fiddler pub near to Manors Metro station and you will come to Argyle Street and View 56 - New Bridge public house. View 57 is in Shieldfield to the north of this spot but as King Charles

house (depicted in the 1960's photograph) is no longer there, it is not worth the detour. Walk south down Argyle Street until you come to Melbourne Street. Cross Melbourne Street and walk along Tower Street to see one of the Town Wall's old towers called Sally-Port or Wall Knoll Tower. The tower is sometimes called Carpenters Tower as a company of ships carpenters used to meet there in the eighteenth century. The town walls used to have 26 gates and towers around its perimeter in the 14th century, but only a handful remain today. With the tower in front of you, turn left and you will see the Gateshead Millennium Bridge. Descend the stone steps to City Road to see view 58 - Barley Mow pub (now called Stereo). The two Geordie actors/entertainers Ant and Dec filmed a scene from the television programme "The Likely Lads" tribute in this pub in 2002.

There aren't any steps to take you down towards the Quayside so you must walk west to the junction with Milk Market and then walk down Milk Market and head for the Waterline public house where you will see view 59. Walk down the Quayside towards the Tyne Bridge and you will pass the new law courts on your right. Here you will see view 60. This is the end of the walk around Newcastle.

Photo: Geoff Phillips 2002

The Principal Photographers

Jack Phillips

My father was born in Bishop Auckland, Co Durham in 1910 and was one of a family of five brothers and sisters. His father was a postman with Bishop Auckland GPO and Jack followed in his father's footsteps by joining the Post Office as a telegraph boy in 1924. In six years he graduated to postman and worked at post offices in Stockton, Thornaby, and Whitley Bay. In the 1940's Jack took up a post as costing clerk with C A Parsons, the steam turbine manufacturer of Byker, a suburb of Newcastle upon Tyne. A few years later he married and lived in a flat on Shields Road in Byker. He took a great interest in the history of Newcastle and started collecting old photographs, sketches and historical notes on the City. Jack died in 1986.

Jim Perry

Jim was born in South Gosforth in 1915 and has lived in Gosforth all of his life. His first job was with the Newcastle upon Tyne Co-op Society and had a number of jobs before serving in the army. After the war he started up his own business selling clothing and household goods. He was a keen photographer and was in great demand to take wedding photographs when people had a little more money to spend. He has been a member of the Gosforth Camera Club for some 44 years. Always interested in the arts, he joined with Scott Dobson and helped to manage the Westgate Art Gallery when it was in Westgate Road, and later, when it moved to Side. Jim took many photographs of Tyneside during the 50's and 60's but was noted for his work in photographing the night life in Newcastle's clubs such as the Downbeat and the Club a'GoGo. He also made recordings of the Jazz ensembles of the day such as the MC5 which was described by Count Basie as the 'Swingiest group in Europe'. Jim is now retired and lives with his wife Margaret in Gosforth.

Steve Wood

Steve Wood was born in Sunderland on 19 June 1912 but moved to Gateshead in 1914. His interest in photography started in about 1925 when he used his family's camera to take photographs of Gateshead. In 1935 he bought his first good quality camera and that's when he started to take the hobby more seriously. In 1945 he took up employment with Turner's photography business at their premises in Pink Lane, Newcastle upon Tyne. Steve retired from Turner's in 1976 but continued his hobby with increased intensity. His slide and print collection now exceeds 8000 in number and in 1996 he decided to donate his collection to the City of Newcastle upon Tyne.

Then and Now Photographs

On the following pages are the "then and now" photographs of Newcastle upon Tyne and its suburbs. In many cases there are links between the old and new views and they are quite good fun to find. For example, it's hard to believe that the two photographs of Percy Street shown below were taken from the same spot, but notice that the building at the top left is the same in both photographs. The building was originally a Jewish synagogue on Leazes Park Road. That building is the link. In some cases there are three or maybe four photographs taken from the same spot but at different times. There may be a link between all four photographs or there may be a link between (a) and (b), then a link between (b) and (c) and so on.

Have fun finding the links. If you run into problems, the answers are given on pages 110 and 111.

Photographs marked * were taken around the turn of the 20th century using a little Paget 3x4 camera. The photographer is unknown.

1.(a) River Tyne looking West 1960's

Photo: Jack Phillips

The origin of the name Tyne is unknown. It may have come from an ancient Celtic word meaning "dissolve" or "flow". At its upper reaches, the river is formed from the North Tyne and South Tyne, and each of these has its own dale. Tyneside is the conurbation on both sides of the river between Newcastle/Gateshead and the sea at Tynemouth/South Shields.

Troubles on Tyne

The River Tyne has experienced some severe winters in its history. In the winter of 1739/40 the Tyne froze over, not in one large sheet but in huge lumps which prevented navigation for several weeks. Heavy snow falls in the winters of 1776 and 1823 cut Tyneside off from the rest of the region for weeks. The roads were blocked by snow drifts, some being 12 feet high, consequently mail coaches could not get through. In 1776 the River Tyne was frozen over from Walker to Newburn. The worst winter, however was that of 1813/14 when the Tyne was covered for two months by a sheet of ice ten inches thick. The tides caused the ice sheet to rise and fall causing the edges to break away from the banks. Gangplanks were installed so that locals could gain access to the ice floe. Booths for selling cakes and fruit were set up on the ice and skating competitions were organised. Newspapers of the day record that the town's Mayor and member of Parliament, Cuthbert Ellison were seen skating on the frozen Tyne. Even football matches took place on this nature-made perfectly flat pitch.

In 1850 the Tyne Improvement Commission was set up which introduced measures to artificially reinforce the river banks by building quays. Dredging of the river also was carried out to improve navigation. The river was much wider and shallower than it is today and there was a constant risk of flooding. Low lying areas of Newcastle were frequently flooded by even a three feet increase in the high tide level. Lower Newcastle, the Quayside, the

1.(b) River Tyne looking West 2002

Photo: Geoff Phillips

Close, the Stockbridge and Scotswood were flooded in 1239, 1782, 1809, and 1815. In 1792 the Stockbridge was washed away. None of these floods compared with the "great flood" on the night of 17th November 1771. At 2 am, after heavy rain, the Tyne was twelve feet higher than the normal spring tide. By daybreak all of the lower town from the Close to the Ouseburn was under water. The middle arch and two other arches on the Gateshead side of the Tyne Bridge had been swept away along with seven shops and houses and their occupants.

Three adults and two children were drowned. The only bridge left standing across the Tyne was at Corbridge.

The Ruins of the Tyne Bridge after the Flood of 1771

2.(a) River Tyne looking East 1960's

Photo: Jack Phillips

2.(b) 2002

Photo: Geoff Phillips

3.(a) Newcastle Quayside looking East 1950's

Photo: Stanley Victor Walton

In the 1950's the Quayside was still a thriving port with ships being loaded and unloaded with cargo around the clock. By the 1970's much larger cargo ships which used containers were in service, and much of the river trade moved to terminals downstream.

In the 1990's a new building programme was introduced which embraced both the Newcastle and Gateshead banks of the Tyne. Instead of warehouses and factories, the plans featured housing, commercial premises and leisure centres.

In 1996 the Millennium Commission announced that it was able to fund 50% of the cost of significant "landmark" projects to mark the coming of the 21st century. The "blinking eye" bridge design emerged as the clear favourite with all the decision making bodies. Assembly of the bridge took place downstream and in November 2000 one of the world's largest cranes, the 10,650 tonne Dutch-built floating crane Asian Hercules II manoeuvred the 850 tonne bridge into position. The world's first ever tilting bridge made its first opening on 28 June 2001. The bridge opened for cyclists and pedestrian traffic on Monday 17 September 2001.

3.(b) Newcastle Quayside looking East 2002

Photo: Geoff Phillips

4.(a) Quayside from Tyne Bridge 1960's

Photo: Jim Perry

4.(b) Quayside from Tyne Bridge 2002

Photo: Geoff Phillips

5.(a) Quayside from Tyne Bridge 1960's

Photo: Jack Phillips

By the mid-fourteenth century Newcastle was the fourth wealthiest town in England. One of the key factors in Newcastle's development had been the reclamation of Sandhill and Quayside from the River Tyne. Before 1200 the Quayside was nothing more than mud and sandbanks. In the fourteenth century clay jetties faced with stone were built which allowed ships to berth and unload their cargo. Many workshops and warehouses were built and this area of the town became the focal point for trade and commerce. Gradually rich merchants moved into the area and had fine houses constructed along Sandhill, The Close, and Side.

By the eighteenth century many of the more wealthy Newcastle citizens were moving away from this part of town to more elegant houses in the higher parts of Newcastle. Nevertheless the Quayside experienced a great increase in trade in the eighteenth century and became *"one of the largest and most commodious wharfs in the kingdom"*.

A new customs house was built in the centre of the Quayside in 1766 and it is the oldest surviving building. along this section of the quay.

5.(b) Quayside from Tyne Bridge 2002

Photo: Geoff Phillips

In 1854 there was a terrible fire which destroyed many of the buildings along the Quayside. In the early hours of 6 October, a fire broke out in Wilsons Worsted factory on the Gateshead riverside area of Hillgate. The fire spread to a chemical factory which suddenly exploded, sending burning fragments of timber across the Tyne to Newcastle's Quayside. Some of the buildings on the Quayside were set on fire. The fire quickly spread, and by dawn 53 people had been killed and 800 families were made homeless.

The 1960's photograph opposite shows the Quayside Sunday market which is claimed to have been established in the twelfth century. Hundreds of stalls are set up along the Quayside stretching from the new law courts to the Swing Bridge. Thousands of people flock to this market every Sunday in the hope of finding a bargain.
R J Charleton in his book "A History of Newcastle on Tyne" describes the market:
"On this portion of the quay is held on Sundays a sort of fair. It is occupied by stalls with gaily covered awnings, mostly owned by Italian vendors of ice cream. The thirsty ones from the crowded Sandhill flock hither for their cold refreshment, which they diversify with ginger beer, lemonade, nuts, oranges, and mussels. The quack doctor and the temperance and religious orators have also their places here."

In 1975 there was an uproar from the market traders when Newcastle City Council threatened to enforce the 1950's Shops Act. The Council proposed to use the act to prevent Sunday trading in household goods, hardware and clothing, and only those stalls selling food and a few assorted items such as aircraft spares and horse fodder would be allowed to trade. Perhaps it was the Council's way of doing something about the many complaints it had received about the market's alleged trade in counterfeit goods.
Newcastle's Quayside Sunday Market continues to attract thousands of visitors.

6.(a) Sandhill 1894

Photo: Newcastle City Libraries

The area close to the Tyne Bridge where the mini-roundabout is situated is called Sandhill. It was so-named because of a mound of silt or sand which would collect at this spot due to a tributary of the River Tyne called the Lort Burn which used to flow down the course of Grey Street and Dean Street. The building on the left of the photograph is the Guildhall. The inside remains from a previous building of 1658 and was the ancient centre of municipal government of the town. For many years the Guildhall was used as the Assize Court of the City and County of Newcastle. It was also used for the guild meetings of the Freemen of the town. In 1794 the building was extensively altered and the front was faced in freestone. The south side of the building was re-faced in 1809 consequently none of the original building is now visible.

The building in the centre of the photograph is the seventeenth century home of Aubone Surtees, who was a wealthy banker and eminent citizen of Newcastle. He

The Guildhall before renovation.

6.(b) Sandhill 2002

Photo: Geoff Phillips

had eight children, the eldest being a beautiful girl called Elizabeth. Further along the Quayside was a chare called Love Lane where a coal merchant called William Scott lived. One of William's three sons was called John and he fell in love with the beautiful Bessie Surtees. Her father strongly disapproved of the match. The loving couple would meet in secret, but when John heard that Bessie's father had arranged for her to marry 63 year old Sir Walter Blackett, he persuaded Bessie to elope with him to Scotland where they were married according to Scottish law in Blackshields. Later they were reconciled with their parents and married according to English law.

John Scott was an ambitious man and studied law until he was called to the bar in 1776. He was noted by his peers as being a brilliant barrister and by 1783 had more work than any of his colleagues. That same year he entered Parliament and in 1788 he

became Solicitor General and was knighted. His career went from strength to strength and he became, in succession, Attorney General, Lord Chief Justice of Common Pleas, Baron Eldon, Lord High Chancellor, and Earl of Eldon. Newcastle's Eldon Square took its name after this famous man from the town's history.

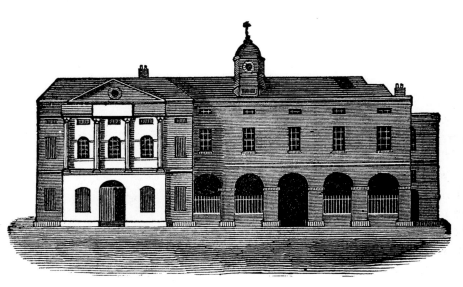

The Guildhall after renovation.

The Newcastle street simply called Side was probably so named because it ran up from the Quayside by the side of the Castle Keep. This photograph above shows how black the stone buildings were in the 1950's due to the smoke pollution from Tyneside's industries.

7(b) Side 2002 *Photo: Geoff Phillips*

8(a) Side 1950's

The fine building seen under the railway arch is Milburn House built in 1906. It was named after Alderman J D Milburn who bought the site and built these fine new offices after a huge blaze had destroyed the printing works and offices of R Robinson and Co. Milburn House was used as a set in the BBC Television's production "Badger".

Photo: Jack Phillips

8(b) Side 2002

Photo: Geoff Phillips

9(a) Grey Street 1930's

Grey Street was named after Charles, Earl Grey who was said to be one of Newcastle's greatest sons and the town's only Prime Minister. He is noted for his work in steering the Reform Bill of 1832 through Parliament. The bill was one of the most important pieces of legislation of its day. On the right is the Theatre Royal which was designed by father and son John and Benjamin Green. Benjamin Green also designed Grey's Monument, seen in the distance.

9(b) Grey Street 2002

Photo: Geoff Phillips

10(a) Grey Street c1900

This photograph was taken a little higher up Grey Street close to the junction with Market Street. To the left of Grey's Monument is the 1821 Presbyterian Church which was known as the "Scotch Church". It was demolished in order to build Emerson Chambers which was completed in 1903.

The organ grinder, complete with monkey, entertains patrons of the Theatre Royal. In those days street entertainers and vendors were expected to stand in the gutter while carrying out their business.

In the photograph below, singer/guitarist Richard J Shulz from Jarrow is seen entertaining the theatre-goers 2002 style on the theatre's new plinth.

10(b) Grey Street 2002

Photo: Geoff Phillips

11(a) Grey Street Cinema c1922

Originally called the Newcastle Picture House when it opened in 1914, the cinema was renamed Grey Street picture house in 1922. It was regarded as Tyneside's first super-cinema. In the picture above, the film "Behind Closed Doors" is being screened. Balcony seats are 1/6 (7.5p) and stalls are 1/- (5p). Walter Barry and his orchestra featured musical interludes. The cinema closed in 1932.

The Eldon Grill is to the left

11(b) Grey Street 2002

Photo: Geoff Phillips

The building now houses a branch of HSBC bank and its
appearance has benefited from the removal of the large
cinema advertising.

12(a) Blackett Street 1960's

Photo: Jack Phillips

This photograph of a deserted Blackett Street in the 1960's is contrasted by the one below which shows the Peruvian band "Golden Empire" treating Newcastle folk to a free concert in the summer sun. The band are using the refurbished plinth of Grey's Monument as a makeshift stage. The cultural birthplace of the band's music is in the many villages and towns clinging to the Andean mountains of Peru. Music is a key component of Peruvian life, the huge variety of pipes, flutes and drums stem from a time when the Incan tribes would use different instruments and different rhythms to establish regional identities.

Photo: Geoff Phillips

12(b) 2001

13(a) Blackett Street 1920's

13(b) 2002

Photo: Geoff Phillips

14(a) Blackett Street 1960's

Photo: Steve Wood

The photograph above shows the west end of Blackett
Street before Eldon Square Shopping Centre was built.

14(b) 2001

15(a) Clayton Street / Nelson Street 1960's

Photo: Steve Wood

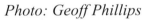

The above photograph shows Clayton Street continuing to meet up with Blackett Street. In the centre of the picture is High Friar Street which ran from Grey's Monument to Newgate Street.

15(b) Clayton Street / Nelson Street 2001

Photo: Geoff Phillips

16(a) Eldon Square 1928

After completing construction of Blackett Street, the famous Newcastle builder Richard Grainger's next task was to build Eldon Square. The corporation bought the site which was an orchard of very old fruit trees, and construction work began in 1825. When Eldon Square was completed in 1831 it was immediately acknowledged as being the city's most graceful development. The statue was added in the 20th century and is an equestrian bronze representation of St George, the Patron Saint of the Northumberland Fusiliers, slaying the dragon. The statue, which was designed by C L Hartwell, is in memory of Newcastle men who died in the two World Wars.

The photograph above was taken in 1928, the year the Tyne Bridge was opened. A rally of very fine motor cars appears to be taking place.

The 1966 photograph was taken on a Sunday morning and the only car around is my late father's Hillman Minx. The Pram Shop is remembered by many Newcastle mams as being the place to shop for their new Silver Cross pram when a new baby arrived.

In 1973 the buildings on two of the three sides of Eldon Square were demolished during the building of the Eldon Square shopping centre. It was argued that there were plenty of other examples of Grainger's architecture in the city. In total, 55 listed buildings were demolished to make way for the shopping centre.

The 2002 photograph shows the square to be very barren. New trees have been planted but most of the grass has been worn away and the concrete area around the monument is now used as a "rink" for skateboarders.

16(b) Eldon Square 1966

16(c) Eldon Square 2002

17(a) Percy Street, 18th Century Shops 1960's

Photo: Jack Phillips

Built in the early 1700's, these old buildings were much-loved by Newcastle folk, but the shops were victims of progress in 1963 when the bulldozers moved in.

17(b) 2002

Photo: Geoff Phillips

18(a) Bourgognes Pub, Newgate Street 1960's

Photo: Jim Perry

Built in 1634, the building in the centre of the photograph above was originally the town jailer's house, but was bought by a French wine merchant, Bourgogne et Fils, in the 1870's. The pub was demolished in the 1970's as part of the Eldon Square Shopping Centre development. This is now possibly the most uninteresting part of town.

18(b) 2002

Photo: Geoff Phillips

19(a) Newgate House, Newgate Street c1962

Photo: Jack Phillips

The photograph shows Newgate House under construction. The ground floor of the building was to be occupied by Moores Supermarket and the vast area below ground was to be Newcastle's brand new dance hall - The Mayfair. In the 2002 photograph a new entertainment and leisure centre is under construction. At the time of writing, "The Gate" is scheduled to open in November 2002.

19(b) 2002

Photo: Geoff Phillips

20(a) Newgate Street 1960's

Photo: Jack Phillips

20(b) Newgate Street 2002

Photo: Geoff Phillips

21(a) Bigg Market c1900

Bigg is a type of coarse barley which farmers brought to this part of the town to sell. The area gradually became a centre for trading in a wide range of goods.

The tall building on the right was Newcastle's Corn Exchange and town hall built 1858-63. There were many people opposed to its construction. In particular, John Dobson said, 'The hideous town hall would ruin the character of what might have been one of the finest streets in the kingdom.' Until 1838 the site of the town hall had been occupied by Middle Street and Union Street, and when they were demolished the Groat Market and Cloth Market faced each other across one of the finest views of St Nicholas Cathedral that Newcastle had ever seen. Nevertheless the town hall was built and when completed it attracted numerous literary criticisms.

A fine new Toon Hall, there's lately been built,
Te sewt mountybank dansors an' singors;
It's a sheym the way the munny's been spilt,
An wor Cooncil hez sair brunt their fingors;

For the room's dull an cawd, tee, an' ghostly an' lang,
An thor fine organ's not worth a scuddick;
An' if frae the gallery ye want te heer a fine sang,
Wey, ye might as weel be in a keel's buddick.

The Bigg Market, Cloth Market, and Groat Market area has always been a lively place with many inns and places of recreation. In 1882 there were 23 pubs, two theatres, 4 beerhouses and three breweries. One of the most famous pubs was The Wheatsheaf, better known as Balmbra's, where Geordie Ridley first sang his composition 'The Blaydon Races' in 1862.

The Bigg Market is still used as a market on certain days of the week. At night the whole area comes alive as hundreds of revellers frequent the many bars, restaurants, and night clubs in the Bigg Market which is now world-famous for being the 'place to party'.

21(b) Bigg Market 1989

Photo: Craig Oliphant

21(c)
2000

Photo:
Geoff Phillips

22(a) Balmbra's Music Hall 1962

It was 1862 when Geordie Ridley sang his composition 'Blaydon Races' in John Balmbra's Wheat Sheaf Music Saloon, Newcastle upon Tyne. The song was an immediate hit and eventually became Tyneside's Anthem. The music hall was nicknamed 'Balmbra's' after its owner, and enjoyed popularity with Newcastle folk until the 1890's when it was rebuilt as a pub and a billiard hall called The Carlton Hotel.

During the late 1950's it was realised that the centenary of the 'Blaydon Races' song was imminent and a joint committee of Newcastle City Council and Blaydon Urban District Council was set up to plan suitable celebrations. Part of these plans was the proposal to reopen Balmbra's as a music hall. A stage was constructed at the far end of the room with a 'pulpit' for the barker (Master of Ceremonies). On the day of Saturday 9th June 1962 crowds gathered outside Balmbra's for the start of a grand parade to re-enact the journey as described in the song, and over 60 bands, 160 floats and 300 people dressed in period costume were seen 'Gannin alang the Scotswood Road.'

In the evening was the first performance of the 20th century Balmbra's music hall; among those appearing on that first night were Alan Mills, Jimmie Campbell, Maureen Cliff, and the Debonaires. The barker was

Benny Cunningham and the music hall had their very own can-can girls. The photograph below shows (clockwise) Mary Reynolds, George Knowles, Pat Healey, and Norman Shiel, all of whom were regular artists at Balmbra's in the 1960's.

22(b) Balmbra's 2001

The final music hall performance was given in 1981, but in 2000 Balmbra's was "born again" when Leah Bell and her company brought music hall back to Newcastle.

Leah Bell, Eileen Wood and Bob Gladwin thought there was a market for weekly variety shows and were looking for a venue in Newcastle. Eileen remembered the shows at Balmbra's in the 60's and 70's as she had entertained there many times. Leah Bell was also no stranger to Balmbra's as she made her first professional appearance there in the early 60's.

Photo: Geoff Phillips

After making enquiries, they were delighted to learn that the music room at Balmbra's was still intact and available as a venue for their shows. The original stage, which was at the back of the room, as seen in the 1960's photograph, was too small for Leah's show so someone had the brilliant idea of turning the period bar into a stage.

The first show, which featured the well-known north-east comedian, Brendan Healy, took to the stage on 4 April 2000 and I was honoured to be invited to that great opening night. The photograph above shows Leah taking the vocal lead during a big production number. The photograph to the left shows the principal players in the show: Johnny De Little (left), Leah Bell, and Jason King.

Leah considers Balmbra's to be a piece of North-East history. She thinks it should be left as it is, and hopes it will not be turned into yet another "fun pub".

Photo: Geoff Phillips

43

23(a) Blackfriars c1900

The order of Dominican or Black Friars settled in Newcastle upon Tyne in 1239. Sir Peter Scott, the first Lord Mayor of Newcastle upon Tyne, is said to have funded the building of the monastery in the west of Newcastle just inside where the City Wall was later built.

The friary in Newcastle was occasionally visited by Kings of England bringing with them gifts of cloth, wine, corn and money for the friars. Edward Balliol paid homage for the Kingdom of Scotland to Edward III there in 1334.

23(b) 2002 *Photo: Geoff Phillips*

24(a) Blackfriars 1960's

Photo: Jack Phillips

After the dissolution of the monasteries, the friary at Newcastle was sold to the City Council who rented it to the town's trade guilds. By the 1960's the buildings were in a terrible state. The City Council gradually acquired control of all the property again and restoration work began in 1975 and was completed in 1981. Blackfriars now houses several craft workshops, and the offices of the North-East Civic Trust.

Photo: Geoff Phillips

24(b) 2002

25(a) Bath Lane 1960's

Photo: Jack Phillips

The photograph above shows Bath Lane as it joined Westgate Road. To the right are sections of the city wall.

In the mid sixties a night club was opened on Bath Lane called "Change Is" financed by Bob Monkhouse.

25(b) Bath Lane 2002

Photo: Geoff Phillips

26(a) Westgate Road / Bath Lane 1900 *

The building in the centre is the House Carpenters Hall built in the early 1800's for the company of House Carpenters. The company originally occupied the old West Gate itself in the eighteenth century.

26(b) Westgate Road / Bath Lane 2002

Photo: Geoff Phillips

27(a) Westgate Road 1900's

The building on the right of the photograph above is the Pavilion Theatre built in 1903. Throughout its life it alternated between operating as a cinema and live theatre until it finally closed in 1975. Further down Westgate Road is the Newcastle Tyne Theatre, formerly the Opera House, and before that the Stoll Cinema.

27(b) Westgate Road 2002

Photo: Geoff Phillips

28(a) Blenheim Street 1990's

Photo: Jack Phillips

St James Boulevard is Newcastle's new western thoroughfare which connects the new Redheugh Bridge to the centre of town. The building on the right of the photograph below is the Discovery Museum which occupies the splendid 1899 CWS regional headquarters. The museum houses many exhibits which remind us of Newcastle's proud and rich heritage. Admission is free.

28(b) St James Boulevard 2001

Photo: Geoff Phillips

29(a) Two Ball Lonnen c1900

Have you ever wondered why Two Ball Lonnen in the west end of Newcastle was so-named? These two 1900 photographs provide a feasible answer. The original ball finials were removed to Whitfield Hall near Allendale.

29(b) 2002 *Photo: Geoff Phillips*

30(a) Two Ball Lonnen c1900

30(b) 2002

Photo: Geoff Phillips

31(a) West Road near Fox and Hounds, looking West c1898

The West Road or West Turnpike as it was known, follows the course of the Roman Wall.

31(b) 1950's

The modern photographs show that the West Road is no longer a country turnpike but has become a suburban thoroughfare which carried a trolley-bus service in the 1950's.

31(c) 2002

32(a) West Road near Fox and Hounds, looking east c1898

The 1898 view shows the original Fox and Hounds pub. On the right are the grounds of West Acres owned by Benjamin Brown, who was the Chairman of Hawthorn Leslie.

32(b) 1950's

The new Fox and Hounds pub was probably built in the 1920's. It may be seen behind the van on the left of the 1950's photograph. There's my dad's old bike parked against the kerb on the right.

32(c) 2002

33(a) Blackett Street / Percy Street 1960's

Photo: Steve Wood

This part of Newcastle was demolished in the 1970's to be replaced by the Eldon Square Shopping Centre.

33(b) 2000

Photo: Geoff Phillips

34(a) Percy Street 1960's

Photo: Jack Phillips

The Percy Arms in the centre of the photograph took its name from the Percy family who (along with the Nevilles and the House of Lancaster) controlled most of the North of England in the fourteenth century. The Percys and the Nevilles helped overthrow Richard II and put Henry Bollingbroke of the House of Lancaster on the throne as Henry IV.

The photograph below shows the Percy Arms still in business in 2002, but the premises are dwarfed by Eldon Gardens, an extension to the Eldon Square Shopping Centre.

34(b) Percy Street 2002

Photo: Geoff Phillips

35(a) Percy Street 1870

PERCY ST. N/C 1870

35(b) Percy Street 1953

Photo: Jack Phillips

35(c) Percy Street 1960's

Photo: Jim Perry

This superb series of photographs shows Percy Street in four different decades. Photograph (b) was taken at the time of the coronation of Queen Elizabeth II. In the centre of the photograph is the Haymarket Hotel which dated back to 1833. The hotel and the Haymarket ABC cinema were removed in the 1980's for a car park.

35(d) Percy Street 2002

Photo: Geoff Phillips

36(a) Haymarket Bus Station 1960's

Photo: Steve Wood

As the name suggests, the Haymarket is where farmers would bring hay and straw to sell. They would then take refreshment in the Farmer's Rest pub seen on the right of the 1960's photograph.

A new bus station was built in 1995 along with an extension to Marks and Spencer's store.

36(b) Haymarket Bus Station 2002

Photo: Geoff Phillips

37(a) St Thomas Church, Barras Bridge 1920's

This superb view of the Haymarket depicts some very fine motor omnibuses. The bus on the far left has just arrived from Amble, while the one on the right is destined for Ashington. The 2002 photograph shows the controversial "soldier sculpture" and water feature which incorporates 52 concrete figures and cost £1/4m.

37(b) St Thomas Church, Barras Bridge 2002

Photo: Geoff Phillips

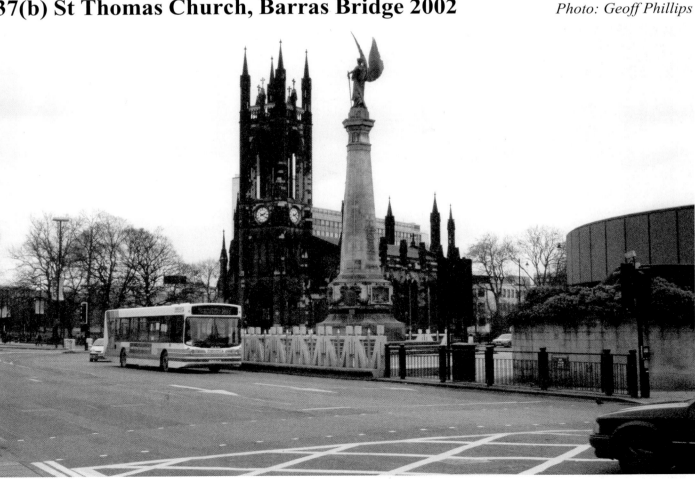

38(a) Town Moor Hoppings 1950's

Photo: Jack Phillips

The 900 acres of grassland to the north of the city which we know as the Town Moor was originally a wood famous for its sturdy oak trees. Many of the houses of old Newcastle and hundreds of ships were built from the trees. The Town Moor, Castle Leazes, and Nun's Moor are said to have been a gift to the Burgesses of Newcastle by Adam of Jesmond in about 1250. King Edward III granted a charter to the town of Newcastle in 1357 confirming possession of the Town Moor as 89 acres of common land. In 1774 an act of Parliament confirmed the City to be owners of the land and gave freemen of the city the right to graze cows on the Moors. In his book "The History of Newcastle upon Tyne" published in 1736, Henry Bourne writes,

Two fairs are kept upon this moor, on the first of August, and eighteenth of October, of which the Tolls,

Booths, Stallage, Pickage, and Courts of Pie Powder, to each of the fairs, were reckoned worth cummunibus Annis in Oliver's time.

There are records that show that horse races were held on the Town Moor in the 1600's but it was not until 1838 that the Northumberland Plate was contested for on the Moor when the third week in June became known as Race Week by Newcastle folk. When Gosforth Park Racecourse was laid out in 1882, racing was transferred there, but Race Week was (and still is) celebrated on the Town Moor with a fair of sideshows, fortune-tellers and roundabouts.

The name "Hoppings" is derived from the hopping or dancing which took place at old fairs.

38(b) Town Moor Hoppings 1950's

Photo: Jack Phillips

The Hoppings is still a major event in the North-East and showmen travel from all over the country to attend. It is said that The Hoppings is the largest non-permanent fair in the world covering 30 acres.

38(c) Town Moor Hoppings 2001

Photo: Geoff Phillips

39(a) Haymarket Bus Station 1960's *Photo: City Repro, City of Newcastle upon Tyne*

A short bus ride from the Town Moor returns you to the Haymarket. The pair of photographs show the remarkable changes which have occurred in this part of Newcastle. In the centre of the 2002 photograph is the Callers clock.

39(b) Haymarket Bus Station 2002

Photo: Geoff Phillips

40(a) Vine Lane 1900 *

Vine Lane is a much forgotten street which runs from the top of Northumberland Street to John Dobson Street. Bookless & Co, the popular chain of fruit and vegetable merchants, may be seen in the early photograph. Further down Vine Lane are the premises of A Beach - Servant's Registry. The three "squaddies" are probably heading back to Fenham Barracks.

40(b) 2002 *Photo: Geoff Phillips*

41(a) Northumberland Street 1966

Photo: Jack Phillips

On the right of the 1966 photograph is the Maykway, Newcastle upon Tyne's first ever Chinese restaurant. In the centre is Wilson and Carter's milliners and haberdashery shop. Children were always fascinated by the system of wooden carriages which ran on overhead rails to transport the money from each sales point to the cashier in the accounts department.

The trolley buses ceased operating in Newcastle in 1966.

41(b) Northumberland Street 2001

Photo: Geoff Phillips

42(a) Northumberland Street 1900 *

Hodgson's garage on the right of the photograph heralds the age of the motor car in Newcastle by advertising a 24 hour breakdown service while two doors down at Nos

115 to 117 Northumberland Street, Armstrong and Co are proud to trade in guns, rifles and revolvers as well as "dog goods", cutlery, bags, and all outdoor sports goods.

42(b) Northumberland Street 2002

Photo: Geoff Phillips

43(a) Finlay & Co Ltd, Northumberland Street 1960's

Photo: Jack Phillips

43(b) 2002

Finlay's tobacconists in the centre of the 1960's photograph occupied one of the earliest remaining buildings on Northumberland Street at the time.

To the right of Finlay's is an elegant building constructed in the early 1900's as a branch of Boots the Chemist. The company had a policy of designing their shop fronts so as to incorporate statues of famous local characters. Those chosen for Newcastle's branch were Thomas Bewick, Harry Hotspur, Sir Thomas Marley and Roger Thornton.

Photo: Geoff Phillips

44(a) Blackett Street / Northumberland Street 1900 *

The terrace on the corner and along Blackett Street are   some of Richard Grainger's earliest buildings in Newcastle.

44(b) Blackett Street / Northumberland Street 2002

Photo: Geoff Phillips

45(a) Amos Atkinson's Shop, Northumberland Street 1897 *

This is one of my favourite photographs and shows Northumberland Street at the time of Queen Victoria's Diamond Jubilee.

In the eighteenth century Northumberland Street was mainly residential. R J Charleton, in his book "A History of Newcastle on Tyne" described this street as,

"Quiet, old unpretentious Northumberland Street, which begins outside where Pilgrim Street gate stood, is formed of brick houses; few of them large, but mostly of the old-fashioned, plain, comfortable class which were built during the last century" (eighteenth century)

During the nineteenth century many of the houses were converted into shops and the street became more of a business thoroughfare. By the time of the second photograph Northumberland Street was firmly established as a retail centre of the city. The flags are flying once more to celebrate the coronation of George VI who became King when his brother Edward VIII abdicated in 1936.

Amos Atkinson's early nineteenth century building was decorated with fancy plasterwork in 1953 to celebrate the Coronation of our present Queen. This decorative treatment, now painted white, can clearly be seen in the 2002 photograph (c). 2002 was the year of Queen Elizabeth II's golden jubilee.

45(b) Amos Atkinson's Shop, Northumberland Street 1937

45(c) 2002

Photo: Geoff Phillips

46(a) Northumberland Street 1930's

This is another view of Northumberland Street taken in an era when motor vehicles were competing with the electric trams for road space on this busy thoroughfare. Northumberland Street had to carry the main north-south A1 trunk traffic as well as local traffic. Nevertheless there seems to be no restriction on parking. On the right is Cook's Corner named after the travel agent situated there. Thomas Cook could be described as the "inventor" of the package holiday.

By the time of the 1950's photograph the trams have gone and been replaced by trolley buses. The rather tatty buildings on the corner of Northumberland Street and Blackett Street have been replaced by the fine white tiles of Burton House. The corner site was occupied by Burton the tailor and the jewellers I Samuel were trading next door. The premises of F W Woolworth may be seen to the left of the trolley bus and Fenwick's department store towers above the trolley.

When John Dobson Street was built in the 1970's it relieved much of the congestion on Northumberland Street. The pavements were widened and traffic restrictions were imposed, but it wasn't until 1998 that Northumberland Street was given over entirely to pedestrians. However the intense north-south pedestrian traffic on a busy Saturday morning can sometimes make the short cross-trip from Fenwick's to W H Smith very difficult.

The 2002 photograph shows Monument Mall on the left, completed in 1992.

Retail names on Northumberland Street Then and Now
Fenwick
Lowe and Moorhouse
Callers
Boots the Chemist
Robson's furniture
C & A Modes
Barry Noble (fruit and vegetable retailer)
Littlewoods
Marks and Spencer
W H Smith
J Bacons and Sons (photographers)
Alderson and Brentnall (music)
A Bookless and Co (fruiterers)
Maynard's (confectioners)
Jackson the Taylor
Woodhouse

46(b) Northumberland Street 1950's

46(c) Northumberland Street 2002

Photo: Geoff Phillips

47(a) Pilgrim Street 1950's

In the middle ages, pilgrimages were fashionable among the more religious and well-off English folk. Pilgrims travelling from the south to visit the Chapel of the Blessed Mary at Jesmond would enter Newcastle through a gate in the town wall which became known as Pilgrims' Gate. Weary from their journey, many Pilgrims would find lodgings in the many inns on the street leading to Pilgrims' Gate and the street became known as Pilgrim Street.

Peaceful and pleasant are the memories which crowd upon us as we survey this ancient street. Turmoil and warfare have small place in its records, and even commerce, with its noisy if peaceful bustle, has not flourished here as in other parts of the town. Its very name brings thoughts of peace and devotion amidst surrounding strife, for it reminds us of those who once trod it, on their way to worship at the, Chapel of Our Lady at Jesmond, secure and unmolested by virtue of their holy mission, in an age of bloodshed and violence. It carries us back into the old time when the pilgrims way was but a footpath, leading along the rising ground between two pleasant valleys, when

seen at intervals between the stems of the trees and through the clustering underwood, sparkled and gleamed in the sun the waters of the Lort and Erick Burns, and when the pilgrims might well have sung, as did John Bunyan's Christian and Hopeful-

" Behold ye how these crystal streams do glide, To comfort Pilgrims by the highway side. "

(Extract from R J Charleton's book "A History of Newcastle on Tyne")

Pilgrims Gate which was situated at the junction of Pilgrim Street and Blackett Street

47(b) Pilgrim Street 2002

Photo: Geoff Phillips

The two photograph were taken looking south and show the junction with Market Street. On the left is the Odeon cinema which was opened in 1931 under the name Paramount. In the 1950's it was the first cinema in the City to equip for Cinemascope and showed "The Robe" starring Richard Burton for five weeks in 1954.

The tall white building at the corner is Carliol House built for the North East Electricity Supply Company in 1927. It is a magnificent structure built in Portland Stone which was very fashionable at the time. On the ground floor were the "Electricity Board" showrooms where my mother used to take me when she was looking for new domestic appliances in the 1950's. I remember that the showrooms were staffed by "canny" Geordie women with whom my mam could relate.
"This is a really good washer, I've got one myself at home," the sales lady would say which really helped my mam to make a difficult decision when spending what was then a small fortune on a new electric washing machine.

The building in the fifties photograph with the flagpole is the Central Police Station, Magistrates Court and Fire Station built in 1931. It recently attained "listed" status.

On the opposite side of Pilgrim Street to the cinema are some of the beautiful buildings constructed by Grainger in the 1830's. The building next to the trolleybus was occupied by the Tyne Temperance Hotel where visitors to Newcastle could stay in the comforting knowledge that an atmosphere of sobriety would be maintained at all times.

In the 1960's "Our Friends in the North" sullied the fine line of Pilgrim Street by giving planning permission to the construction of Commercial Union House which is seen in the 2002 photograph jutting out over the southbound carriageway.

48(a) New Bridge Street 1960's

Photo: Steve Wood

The photograph above was taken from the concrete deck which was built over John Dobson Street in an effort to segregate pedestrian traffic from road traffic. Most of the deck was demolished in the late 1990's.

The new premises of the Newcastle Building Society seen on the right of the 2001 photograph were designed to harmonise with the former Lying-in Hospital designed by John Dobson.

48(b) 2002 *Photo: Geoff Phillips*

49(a) Carliol Street 1960's

Photo: Jim Perry

Carliol Street is to the right and New Bridge Street is in the foreground. Grossmans hardware store supplied Novocastrians with all the materials for home improvement in an age before the out of town DIY warehouses came on the scene. The 2002 photograph below shows John Dobson Street which was extended southwards in the 1990's.

49(b) John Dobson Street 2002

Photo: Geoff Phillips

50(a) New Bridge Street 1960's

Photo: Jack Phillips

The photograph above shows New Bridge Street in the swinging 60's. The Trafalgar and Lord Nelson pubs on Trafalgar Street competed for business for a few years before the bulldozers moved in and rased this part of town to the ground in order to build the Central Motorway East. The sketch opposite shows Pandon Dene which ran approximately where the Warner Brothers cinema complex now stands. New Bridge Street took its name from the bridge seen in the sketch.

Bridge over Pandon Dene.
from painting by James Dewar, 1833.

50(b) 1990

The 1990 picture shows that the construction of the Crest Hotel had effectively bisected New Bridge Street.

Who would have thought that by the year 2000 Newcastle folk would be ice skating on New Bridge Street.

50(c) 2000

51(a) Central Library, New Bridge Street 1960's

Photo: Steve Wood

When the Free Library Act was adopted by Newcastle upon Tyne, it was decided to build the city's central library on New Bridge Street alongside, and harmonising with the splendid architecture of the Mechanics' Institute.. The Free Library was opened on 7 December 1881.

The 1969 view shows the new Central Library, designed by Sir Basil Spence, and completed in 1968. John Dobson Street, built in 1970, is shown to the right of the library and extended from St Mary's Place to New Bridge Street. It was built as a bypass to the busy Northumberland Street. On the left of the 1969 photograph is the Burton House pub and Boydells toy shop.

The 2002 photograph shows the city's new Blue Carpet art project. Thomas Heatherwick Studio is the team behind the innovative Blue Carpet design for the first new public space in the city in the twentieth century. Thomas Heatherwick Studio's design was the winning entry in a public competition launched by Newcastle City Council in July 1996 in partnership with local business, Northern Arts and Tyne and Wear Museums. The scheme received its funding from the Arts Lottery Fund and the European Regional Development fund.

The Blue Carpet is a visually thrilling but completely functional urban space; it introduces colour and cohesion to a setting which contains a mix of building types and had no defining character. The purpose-made tiles, the result of considerable research, comprise a durable white resin mixed with recycled glass shards giving a shimmering effect of cool blues. Laid across the square and "riding up" against the gallery, the carpet draws the buildings together and creates an intimate open space for both performance and play. At the edges bollards puncture the surface, preventing vehicular access and creating a safe, secure recreational space for pedestrians.

To form the seating the blue glass tile surface has been peeled back creating benches and voids. The voids are lit providing illumination for the square and a focus for attention.
(The above text is from the City's promotional website)

The Laing Art Gallery may be seen in all three photographs at the right, however the 2002 view shows the gallery's superb new stone and glass frontage. To the right of the office block, out of camera shot is the nightclub Ikon which was originally a dance hall called the Oxford Galleries.

51(b) New Central Library, New Bridge Street c1969
Photo: Jack Phillips

51(c) Blue Carpet 2002
Photo: Geoff Phillips

Photo: Newcastle Chronicle & Journal

The Oxford Galleries on New Bridge Street first opened its doors on Monday 22 June 1925. Music was provided by the London Sonara Band under the direction of Bobbie Hind. The band were billed as having been specially commanded to appear before King George V and Queen Mary. During that first Race Week at the Oxford two dancing experts, Miss Dorothy Drew and Tom Greenwill were also hired to give demonstrations of the latest steps. Dancing was from 7pm until 11pm and the entrance fee was two shillings. Men who felt that their dance steps needed improving could engage the services of one of the professional lady hostesses in the "pen" for a fee of sixpence per dance.

In the mid 1930's Peter Fielding and his Orchestra provided the music and remained at the Galleries for over 14 years.

The photograph above shows George Evans and his "Symphony of Saxes" in October 1951 playing for a special charity dance to raise funds for the Newcastle Police Widows and Orphans Fund.

George is seen top left conducting the orchestra and it is thought that the singer was called Eve.

Don Smith and his Orchestra took over in 1956 along with singer Kay Rouselle. The band continued to play music for ballroom dancing until the late 60's when the Oxford was converted into a nightspot called Tiffany's. However, Don did make a comeback in the 80's when his orchestra played music for afternoon "tea dances" at Tiffany's.

OXFORD GALLERIES

2/6   TONIGHT   2/6
Old Time, 7 till 11.

FRIDAY: Jackson   the   Tailors,
8 p.m. till 1 a.m. 7/6
SATURDAY: 7.30 p.m. till 11.30
p.m. 6/-

AFTERNOON DANCE
SATURDAY: 3—5.30 .... 2/6

DON SMITH AND HIS ORCHESTRA

52(b) Ikon-Diva 2002

Photo: Darren Scott

Tiffany's was renamed Studio, and then Ritzy's before acquiring its present name Ikon-Diva in 1995. The club now caters for 18 to 28 year-olds and the music played is known as "commercial dance". Manager Iain McKay admitted that some things haven't changed since the "Oxford Galleries" days. Young people still come here to find a partner and the "chemistry" is the same now as in the 1950's. Lads still come to "pull" a girl, but now girls can ask lads for a dance.

"Many people met their partners at the Oxford and now their kids come to Ikon to meet someone," said Iain, "that's the historic beauty of the place. We still have the 'kissing booths' upstairs just like the Oxford days"

The doors at Ikon open at 9:30pm and the entrance fee is typically £6. Lads are requested not to wear trainers or have visible tattoos. Regular patrons are encouraged to become members and are given plastic cards which are swiped on entry and notch up points for a free drink. There are seven bars in Ikon where the most popular drinks are "alco-pops". The music is mainly on disc, however, live bands such as Lasgo, JK, Sash, and Ian Van Dahl (the

biggest selling dance artist with four top ten hits) appear at Ikon from time to time. When I visited Ikon in June 2002, the resident DJ Darren Scott was proud to demonstrate Ikon's 33kW sound system which, he explained, is run at 12kW so as to limit the sound level on the dance floor to 95dB in order to comply with the Health and Safety Executive's rules.

A quarter of a million pound laser light show and 25 Golden Scan lighting effect units are controlled by a computer. A live video link transmits television camera images of the dancers onto a huge video screen. If the partying just gets too heavy there's a "chill-out room" where people can get really cool.
The raving continues until 2 am.

Scenes from the cult movie "Get Carter" were filmed in the Oxford Galleries in 1971. The original Tudor Bar, as seen in the film, is still intact although the room is now used as a storeroom. The original Oxford wooden dance floor still exists at Ikon.

53(a) New Bridge Street 1904

New Bridge Street took its name from a new bridge which was built in 1812 across, what was then, a wide and deep dene which ran to the east of the city from Barras Bridge to Pandon. The dene was described as a bonny place with gorgeous gardens lining the ravine. Instead of the shriek of railway whistles, the sweet songs of birds filled the air. A sketch of the dene in 1833 is shown on page 76.

The railways certainly took over this part of town in the nineteenth century as the sign above the remnants shop confirms. The shop occupied the corner where Oxford Street and Picton Place converged. Oxford Street was to the left of the shop and Picton Place (which was

demolished to build more railway sidings) was to the right. The date of the photograph may be accurately confirmed as being 1904 by the advertisement for evening classes at Rutherford College seen at the extreme right of the photograph.

This date of 1904 gives the picture an historic significance as it was the date that Tyneside's new electric train service came into operation. Trains departed from New Bridge Street Station (seen to the left of the tram) to Benton initially and, soon after, electrification was extended to Tynemouth and Whitley Bay.

By 1919 more railway sidings had been laid at this spot and a goods station built to the west of Shieldfield Green. The goods station was heavily bombed during the second world war and stood in ruins for the next two decades. In the 1970's this area was cleared for the construction of the Central Motorway East. The 2002 photograph shows the roundabout which connects the motorway to Durant Road and New Bridge Street East. A Warner Brothers cinema complex and car parks now occupy the area where a goods station once stood.

53(b) New Bridge Street 1960's

Photo: City Repro

The garage on the right of the photograph above was owned by the Travers family. The Geordie actor Bill Travers (who married Virginia McKenna) appeared in the film "Geordie" in the 1950's.

53(c) Central Motorway East 2002

Photo: Geoff Phillips

54(a) Oxford Street 1960's

Photo: Steve Wood

This is another view of Oxford Street looking north towards Ellison Place. Newcastle Polytechnic (now the University of Northumbria) may be seen in the distance.

The modern photograph shows Durant Road which connects John Dobson Street to the roundabout above the Central Motorway East.

54(b) Durant Road 2002

Photo: Geoff Phillips

55(a) Oxford Street 1960's

Photo: Steve Wood

Oxford Street connected Ellison Place with New Bridge Street and was demolished to build Durant Road leading to the Central Motorway East. The photograph above was taken from a spot close to the Church of the Divine Unity in Ellison Place. It's almost impossible to take a photograph from the same place today due to a pedestrian bridge, so I have used "poetic licence" for the 2001 shot and taken the photograph from the east end of Ellison Place which overlooks the Central Motorway East. The photograph makes for a more dramatic effect when compared with the 1960's photo.

55(b) Central Motorway East 2002

Photo: Geoff Phillips

56(a) New Bridge Public House, Argyle Street 1966

Photo:
Jack Phillips

John Fitzgerald became the owner and licensee of the New Bridge public house in 1876. It was the beginning of an impressive career in the licensed premises business in North-East England. John Fitzgerald became Lord Mayor of Newcastle in 1914 and was knighted in 1920. The picture above shows the New Bridge Street goods station which was heavily bombed in the Second World War. The site is now occupied by a cinema complex.

56(b) 2002

Photo:
Geoff Phillips

57(a) King Charles House, Shieldfield 1960

During the English Civil War in the 1640's King Charles was interned in Newcastle. Occasionally he was allowed to play golf on Shieldfield Green and rested at a house there. The house, which may be seen in front of the block of flats, survived until July 1961 when Newcastle Council decided to demolish it in order to further develop the housing in Shieldfield.

Photo: Jack Phillips

57(b) 2001
Photo: Geoff Phillips

58(a) Barley Mow, City Road 1920

City Road – top of Milk Market N/c 1920

58(b) Stereo 2001

Photo: Geoff Phillips

The Barley Mow pub shown in the centre of the picture opposite is often referred to as the New Barley Mow by pub historians, as records show there to be a pub called the Barley Mow in this spot as long ago as 1827. Records also show there were two pubs in close proximity, both bearing this name. The pub shown in the photograph was the high Barley Mow and a second pub called the low Barley Mow traded on Sandgate. A brewery, malt storage buildings, and stables occupied the land in between. The low Barley Mow closed in 1905 but the other survived until the 1970's.

The building then became derelict but was rescued by an enterprising Geordie in 1979 when Stuart Beveridge used his life savings to buy the property. He transformed it into a French restaurant which he called Beveridges.

In 1995 the building was given a major make-over and reverted to a pub once more under the name of the Fog and Firkin. The pub was refurbished in 2002 and renamed "Stereo". It was used as a set in a scene from the Ant and Dec's Tribute to The Likely Lads screened by BBC1 in 2002.

The pub now enjoys splendid views of the Gateshead Millennium Bridge which opened for cyclists and pedestrian traffic on Monday 17 September 2001. The bridge is a unique design which can tilt to allow river traffic to pass underneath. The tilting action is described by the designers, Wilkinson Eyre Architects / Gifford & Partners, as like "the blinking of an eye". The bridge was built by Harbour and General, a Gateshead based construction company. It cost £22 million, almost half being paid for by Lottery money through the Millennium Commission.

The tall building behind the Millennium Bridge is Baltic - Gateshead's Centre for Contemporary Art which opened on 13 July 2002. Architect Dominic Williams redesigned this former Baltic Flour Mills, a disused 1950's grain warehouse, into a leading international contemporary visual arts space, one of the biggest temporary art spaces in Europe. The Director of the centre, Sune Nordgren, describes Baltic as a meeting place where people can come together; a place where exciting things are created, where nothing is impossible. The centre houses five different galleries, three artists' spaces and a performing arts space. It also boasts a media lab, a cinema, library, retail outlets and two restaurants; the rooftop restaurant having amazing views of Tyneside. Admission to Baltic is free.

59(a) The Tyne Public House, Quayside 1960's

59(b) The Waterline Public House, Quayside 2002

60(a) Quayside 1920's

The Tyne Bridge was under construction when the above photograph was taken as can be seen above the ship on the left.

60(b) Quayside 2002

61(a) Tyne Tees Television, City Road 1960

Photo: Jack Phillips

Tyne Tees Television started transmitting in January 1959 from two converted warehouses on City Road. Channel 8 soon became a hit as we were enthralled with programmes that "we wanted to watch", not programmes "they" wanted us to watch. The Egypt Cottage pub next door was nicknamed "Studio 5" by staff of Tyne Tees.

61(b) 2002 *Photo: Geoff Phillips*

62(a) Egypt Cottage c1900

City Road is described as "The New Road" in R J Charleton's "History of Newcastle on Tyne" (1893). In Charleton's book he describes this part of the New Road as Egypt, a name it received on account of the erection of temporary wooden granaries here in 1796 which were used to store grain in the manner of the Pharoahs. The granaries were used as barracks in 1803.

Rich merchants were said to live in a row of elegant houses here which were given the modest name Egypt Cottages.

In his book "Heavy Nights - A History of Newcastle's Public Houses", Brian Bennison records that an Egypt pub on this site may have been Newcastle's first licensed public house. Records show there to be an Egypt Inn here in the early eighteenth century and later an Egypt Tavern. The pub shown in the photographs was built in 1873 and was given its first major make-over at the turn of the 20th century. The pub was used as a television set by Tyne Tees for many of their productions such as "The Tube" in the 1980's.

62(b) Egypt Cottage 2002

Photo: Geoff Phillips

63(a) Byker Bank 1966

The Imperial Cinema opened in 1938 and continued to provide entertainment for Byker folk until 1963. It then became a warehouse and was eventually demolished in order to build the new road system bypassing Shields Road. Further downhill is the Bay Horse pub. The 2001 photograph below shows the Metro bridge which takes the trains into Byker Station.

63(b) Byker Bank 2001

*Photo:
Geoff Phillips*

64(a) Shields Road, Byker 1920's

No. 90   Shields Road, Byker.

64(b) Shields Road, Byker 2002

Photo: Geoff Phillips

65(a) Dalton Street, Byker 1960's

Photo: Jim Perry

65(b) Dalton Street, Byker 2002

Photo: Geoff Phillips

66(a) Commercial Road / Oban Road, Byker 1960's

Photo:
Jim Perry

The Co-op store seen on the right is at the corner of Commercial Road and Raby Street. On the opposite corner, on the left of the photograph is the "Middle Club".

The Raby, seen behind the lamppost, started life as a cinema in 1910 but became a bingo hall in 1961. The "Middle Club" was rebuilt at the same time as the Byker Wall housing complex

66(b) 2002

Photo: Geoff Phillips

67(a) Byker Tavern, Byker Bank 1960's

Photo: Jack Phillips

The Byker Tavern (known by locals as the police bar when it was managed by an ex-member of the force) was closed in 1970. Further down Byker Bank was the New Hawk Inn which may be seen above the old-fashioned "keep left" sign. Not a single pub remains trading on Byker Bank in 2002.

67(b) Byker Bank 2002

Photo: Geoff Phillips

68(a) Ouseburn 1960's

Photo: Jack Phillips

68(b) Ouseburn 2002

Photo: Geoff Phillips

69(a) Crawford's Bridge, Ouseburn 1960's

Photo: Jack Phillips

Said to be the oldest bridge in the City, Crawford's Bridge in the foreground was built in the mid-1700's. It took its name from Thomas Crawford who owned many of the properties in the area including Crawford's Row, seen in the background. I would like to thank Alan Fearon for his help in making this "Rags to Riches" photo-fantasy possible. His prestige car business is on Foundry Lane just a few yards from where this photograph was taken.

69(b) 2000

70(a) Shields Road, Byker 1960's

Photo: Jim Perry

This view shows the west end of Shields Road just before Byker Bridge. Jim Perry, who took the photograph, was the very proud owner of the Humber motor car seen in the picture.

70(b) Shields Road, Byker 2002

Photo: Geoff Phillips

71 Flora Robson Playhouse, Benton Bank, Jesmond 1960's

Photo: Jack Phillips

First known as the Dinky when it opened in 1921, the theatre had a canvas roof and seats on stone terraces. It subsequently became the Jesmond Pavilion then, in 1926 the Playhouse, and eventually the Newcastle Repertory Theatre. Dame Flora agreed to let her name be used to promote the theatre in the 1960's but it finally closed for business in 1971.

Dame Flora Robson was born in South Shields on 28th March 1902. She studied at RADA (Royal Academy of Dramatic Arts) and came to film via a distinguished stage career both in London's West End and occasionally Broadway in America. She appeared in many films where her strong character portrayals and distinctive looks made her presence unmistakable.

72(a) Flora Robson Playhouse, Benton Bank, Jesmond 1960's

Photo:
Jack Phillips

72(b) 2002

Photo: Craig Oliphant

73(a) Jesmond Road 1920's

Jesmond became a popular place to live in Victorian times. This area of Jesmond is known as Cradlewell after the cradle shaped horse trough which may still be seen today further down the road on the right. This part of Jesmond Road was bypassed in the 1990's by the coast road extension seen on the right of the 2002 photograph.

73(b) Jesmond Road 2002

Photo: Geoff Phillips

74(a) High Street, Wallsend 1920's

The only way I was able to discover where 74(a) was taken was to zoom in on the street nameplate "The Avenue" which is just to the left of the trees. I was then able to find a link between the old and new photographs.

74(b) High Street, Wallsend 2002

Photo: Geoff Phillips

75(a) Tyne View, Howdon 1923

This part of tyneside was once a thriving community with many of the locals gaining employment with the River Tyne

Commissioners' workshops on the right of the picture. The entrance to the Tyne Tunnel is behind the trees in the 2002 photograph.

75(b) Tyne View, Howdon 2002

Photo: Geoff Phillips

76(a) New Quay, North Shields 1920's

This was once a very busy part of North Shields as the ferry terminal is located just behind the buildings on the left.

76(b) New Quay, North Shields 1990's   *Photo: Craig Oliphant*

77(a) North and South Shields 1950's

Photo: Jack Phillips

The crane on the left of the photograph above marks the location of Brigham's dock which operated the largest dry dock on the north-east coast. The area is now a new housing development called Coble Landing.

77(b) North and South Shields 2001

Photo: Geoff Phillips

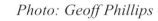

78(a) Mouth of the Tyne 1950's

Photo: Jack Phillips

These two photographs were taken from the same spot   as 77, only looking east. In the foreground is Clive Street.

78(b) Mouth of the Tyne 2001

Photo: Geoff Phillips

The Links Between the Old and New Photographs

If the links are obvious, they are not included in this list.

1. Tyne Bridge and Gateshead Millennium Bridge
The most obvious link is the Tyne Bridge but further links are the Baltic on the left and the Malmaison Hotel (formerly the Co-operative Warehouse) on the right.

2. River Tyne Looking East
The link is the Spillers warehouse in the distance on the right.

3. Quayside Looking East
The link may be the spire or chimney in the distance.

4. Quayside From Tyne Bridge
Dozens of links here - see how many you can find. St Anne's church spire on the right may be one you have missed.

12. and 13. Blackett Street
Notice that the stone facades of Nos 18, 22, and 30 Blackett Street have been saved and integrated into the new Monument Mall complex.

14. Blackett Street
The link is the IBM building which may be seen poking above the Eldon Square building in the 2001 photograph.

15. Clayton Street
The links are Grainger's fine stone buildings of Grainger Market on the right and Nelson Street in the centre.

16. Eldon Square
The link between photo (a) and (b) is the Pram Shop building on the left. The statue of George slaying the dragon links all three photographs.

19. Newgate Street
The link is the Co-op store at the right.

21. Bigg Market
The curved stonework at the top left is one of the links between (a) and (b). The two buildings to the right of the Half Moon pub in (b) may be seen in (a). The building with the curved attic windows in the centre of the photograph is the same in (a), (b), and (c).

22. Balmbra's Music Hall
Notice the ceiling is the same in both views and a section of the curved bar may be seen at the bottom left of the 1962 photograph.

24. Blackfriars
I found it difficult to line up the new shot with the old, until I saw the coat of arms carved in stone and set between the upstairs windows on the left.

27. Westgate Road
The link is the Tyne Theatre in the centre of the photographs.

28. St James Boulevard
Notice the spires of the towers of the Discovery museum are poking above the pub roof on the 1960's photograph.

29 & 30. Two Ball Lonnen
The two balls aren't the same but is the stone cottage the same in both old and new pictures? Sue Hawksley of the Ashton Court Nursing Home thinks not because the house used to be half the size and was only extended 12 years ago.

35. Percy Street
The link between (a) and (b) is the Haymarket pub. The link between (b), (c), and (d) is the Newcastle Breweries building.

40. Vine Lane
The stone building right at the far end of Vine Lane may be the link.

42. Northumberland Street
The Nobles Amusements building on the right is the link.

44. Blackett Street
The T and G Allan building on the left is the link.

45. Amos Atkinson, Northumberland Street
The link is Amos Atkinson's shop.

46. Northumberland Street
The link between all three photographs is Fenwick's store.

49. John Dobson Street
The links are the Lying-in hospital on the left and the building with balustrades on the right.

50. New Bridge Street
The link between (a) and (b) is the BSM building. The link between (b) and (c) is the hotel.

53. New Bridge Street
The link between (a) and (b) is the building under the church spire in (a) - the building may be seen behind the petrol sign in (b). The church spire links (a) to (c). The blocks of flats link (b) to (c).

54. Oxford Street / Durant Road
The links are Durant Hall in the centre of (a), the University of Northumberland's Ellison Building, and the terraced houses on the left.

55. Oxford Street
The links are the multi-storey car park in Gateshead, the Tyne Bridge, and the spire of All Saints Church.

58. City Road
The Barley Mow pub seen in the centre of (a) is the link.

63. Byker Bank
The blocks of flats in the distance are the link.

64. Shields Road
The links are Beavans shop on the left and the pub and shops on the right.

65. Dalton Street
The link is the block of flats - under construction in (a).

67. Byker Bank
The house at the foot of Byker Bank in (b) may be seen in (a).

68. Ouseburn
Notice the stone steps on the left and the pigeon loft are the same.

72. Benton Bank
Although the tree on the right has grown a lot in (b) it is the same tree as in (a).

74. High Street, Wallsend
The chimney stack above and slightly to the right of the steamroller is the link.

76. New Quay, North Shields
The buildings on the left and in the centre are the same.

77. North and South Shields
There are lots of links such as the bridge, the block of flats in South Shields and the buildings on Clive Street.

78. Mouth of the Tyne
The buildings on Clive street.

The Cycling Craze in Bigg Market, Newcastle upon Tyne 1897

Other books by Geoff Phillips

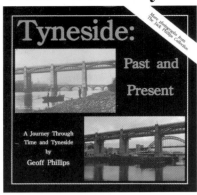

Tyneside: Past and Present

Over 100 photographs of Tyneside as it used to be alongside views of the present day. Intriguing facts and information about each photograph along with a descriptive journey around Tyneside which shows the reader the views in the order as they appear in the book.

Price: £6.95   ISBN 0 9522480 0 X

Tyneside Pubs: Past and Present

Tyneside Pubs: Past and Present is another book in the hugely successful Past and Present series. It presents the reader with a nostalgic pictorial pub-crawl through time and Tyneside. More photographs from the Jack Phillips Collection show pubs in Newcastle and its suburbs as they were in days gone by along with modern photographs showing how things have changed. A pub quiz is included to test the reader's knowledge of bygone boozers.

Price: £6.95   ISBN 0 9522480 2 6

Old Pubs of Newcastle

A collection of photographs of pubs from the past.
Why remember old pubs of Newcastle? For many Tynesiders the pub is their second home, a place to unwind, a place to hear a good story or joke, a venue for a dart's match, a forum for an impromptu discussion on any subject under the sun. The pub is part of the culture of a town or suburb; a sociologist wanting to study a town's ethos might visit a pub for an instant picture of the townspeople's attitudes and way of life. Pubs also form part of the history of a city, its architectural heritage, its styles and fads.

Or maybe its just a place to enjoy a canny pint and a bit crack with your mates.

Price: £4.95   ISBN 0 9522480 4 2

Memories of Tyne Tees Television

A nostalgic look at the early years of the North-East's regional television station to celebrate its 40th birthday

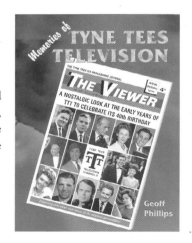

The book 'Memories of Tyne Tees Television' is mainly about the 'Black Brothers Era' (1959 to mid sixties) when Light Entertainment was 'King' and the City Road Studios buzzed with music, singing, dancing and comedy. The book includes many intriguing stories about the programmes and the people and features interviews with Mike Neville, Bill Steel, David Hamilton and many more personalities.

Price: £9.95   ISBN 0 9522480 6 9 (All prices include postage and packing)

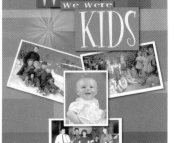

When We Were Kids

Growing up in North-East England in the 1950's and 60's

Making the TV series for Tyne Tees was a labour of love - eight people from widely different backgrounds doing widely different things at the same time all set against the marvellous backdrop of post-war Northern England. In this book Geoff Phillips, who was himself one of our carefully selected octet, has extracted poignant moments in their stories and has also detailed his own upbringing (or dragging up as he might say!) on industrial Tyneside. And all of it illustrated with photographs and memorabilia of those distant days.
The Fifties and Sixties set many trends, both good and bad which continue today. I mean these days youngsters don't know how lucky they are. Now when WE were kids.......

Andy Kluz - Series Presenter

Price: £9.95   ISBN 0 9540174 1 2

All books are obtainable where you bought this book, or by mail order from
G P Electronic Services, 87 Willowtree Ave, Durham City DH1 1DZ.